What is News?

Other books from ELM...

Japanese for Business Communication:
beginner's level - Nakagawa/Takekoshi
Workbook & accompanying two-sided audio cassette. Familiar business & social situations develop a knowledge of the language & culture. 15 graded lessons.
55   Book, A4 wirobound   1 85450 010 4
55T   Audio cassette - 2 sides x 30minutes = 1 hour
55TM Tutor's Manual - exercises, notes etc   1 85450 030 9

Beginner's French for Business - Helena Shaw
A4 workbook of graded exercises and 2 accompanying audio tapes.
78   Book - A4 wirobound   1 85450 021 X
78T   2 Audio cassette tapes, each 2 sides x 30 minutes = 2 hours

Enjeux Débats Expression - M. Le Cunff-Renouard & D.Ditner
Topical issues & essay writing in French. A *unique* combination of information on current issues in French society with learning strategies at 1st year degree level.
25   Book - pbk 320pp.   0 946139 12 1
EFL

Living English: thinking, speaking, writing
Le Cunff Renouard/Ditner/Martin
For advanced students of EFL, LIVING ENGLISH also caters for mature speakers of English - either College students or professionals who want to improve their communication & writing skills. The book's original & effective ways of teaching & learning English is perfectly suited to students engaged in cultural studies programmes.
74   Book   352pp. Autumn, 1993   1 85450 912 1

What
is
News

?

John Venables

ELM Publications

This first edition of **What is News?** is published September, 1993 by ELM Publications, Seaton House, Kings Ripton, Huntingdon, PE17 2NJ. (Tel.04873-254 or 238 Fax 04873-359).

Printed by St Edmundsbury Press, Bury St Edmunds, Suffolk, England. Bound by Woolnough Bookbinding, Express Works, Church Street, Irthlingborough, Northants, England.

ISBN 1 85450 052 X

British Library Cataloguing-in-Publication Data.

A catalogue record for this publication is available from The British Library.

CONTENTS

The Author

John Venables is a freelance broadcast journalist and journalism instructor. Born in 1954, he read modern history and politics at Southampton University. He joined the BBC in 1984, and spent the next five years working as a reporter and producer in local radio. In 1990 he was appointed as the BBC's first bi-media regional science correspondent, based in Cambridge. He currently works as a consultant for BBC World Service Training in Romania, and also runs media training courses for industry, local authorities and educational institutions.

Acknowledgements

The research for this book was carried out with the help of a BP Press Fellowship at Wolfson College, Cambridge. I am indebted to Bill Kirkman MBE, Director of the Press Fellowship Programme, and to British Petroleum plc, for their generosity and support. My particular thanks must go to Dr Phyllis Lee of the Department of Biological Anthropology at the University of Cambridge for introducing me to the Machiavellian hypothesis, and for her patient explanations, suggestions and criticism. I am also grateful to the many other people who helped me with ideas or practical assistance, especially: Dr Ray Abrahams, Department of Social Anthropology, University of Cambridge; Andrew Denwood, Producer, BBC Special Current Affairs; Sarah Fuller, Chief Instructor, BBC Radio Training; Professor Tom Goldstein, Dean of the Faculty of Journalism, University of California, Berkeley; Arnold Miller, Head of Centre, BBC East; Dr Sarah-Jane Richards, Department of Medicine, University of Cambridge; Alison Sargent, Assistant Editor, BBC Radio Cambridgeshire; Professor Philip Schlesinger, Department of Film and Media Studies, University of Stirling; James Serpell, Director of the Companion Animal Research Group in the Department of Veterinary Medicine, University of Cambridge; Professor Hugh Stephenson, Department of Journalism, City University; Ivor Yorke, former Head of BBC Journalism Training.

INTRODUCTION

Journalists are directly responsible for the news we see and hear on TV and radio and in the newspapers. They decide which stories are used and which are left out, and, through the way stories are presented, they decide the significance the public attaches to world events.

What criteria do the news producers use to make such important judgements on our behalf? Strangely, the answer is anything but clear. Ask most journalists what news is and the response will be a tentative list of vague rules of thumb dimly remembered from student days.

This curious ignorance stems both from the historical status of the profession and the way journalists perceive their own role.

Despite the recent boom in computerised studios, modem links and the other paraphernalia of hi-tech news rooms, journalism is still regarded as a craft and not a science. News evaluation is taught as a craft skill, which in practice means that the trainee journalist is expected to acquire a 'nose for news' through a mixture of experience and advice passed on from more senior colleagues.

Such an approach may have worked in the past, because the trainee was not expected to make important editorial decisions until this process of professional 'osmosis' had taken place. But the apprenticeship system is a luxury editors can no longer afford. Particularly in local radio, relatively inexperienced journalists are required to make important news judgements within days of starting work on the news desk. To do so effectively, they need to know what news is, they need to understand the influences which affect the way news is processed, and they need to have a clear idea of what impact their stories are likely to have on the audience.

Over the last forty years media analysts have developed a number of theories which attempt to explain the inner workings of the news operation. Some of these models are drawn from field work and direct observation of what actually happens in the newsroom; others are more theoretical and are based on the application of sociological or linguistic theory to news analysis.

Neither approach has won much attention or favour from professional journalists. At one level there is a conceit among hacks that writing is - as the poet Dylan Thomas put it - a 'craft and sullen art', the arcane mysteries of which should not be sullied by rational analysis. There is also a more practical prejudice: working journalists are in general wary of theory and what they dismiss as 'sociological jargon'. It is widely felt that theoretical models do not reflect real life and are largely irrelevant to the practicalities of the news-gathering operation.

This book attempts to bridge the credibility gap by bringing together all the mainstream ideas on news evaluation and assessing their relevance in terms of what actually happens in the newsroom. It also proposes an alternative model which uses new ideas about human motivation to answer many outstanding puzzles about the nature of news. Above all, it offers a practical guide on how to select, write and present stories so they will have maximum impact on the audience.

CHAPTER 1

"MAN BITES DOG"

"News is about people ... news is about what they talk about down at the local pub ... news is something someone wants kept secret ...

There are as many definitions of news as there are journalists, old saws which distil the wit and wisdom of generations of reporters. But while such handy 'one-liners' may often contain more than a grain of truth, they're not much help in explaining what distinguishes news from mere information.

Perhaps the most frequently quoted attempt at an answer is credited to John B. Bogart, city editor of *The New York Sun* between 1873 and 1890:

"When a dog bites a man, that is not news, because it happens so often. But if a man bites a dog, that is news."[1]

"MAN BITES DOG"

Like many examples of journalistic lore Bogart's aphorism rings true, but as a definition it fails dismally. It tells us nothing about the essential nature of news, and doesn't even explain itself in its own terms. Why should the rarity of an event make it newsworthy?

Just after the Second World War the first Royal Commission on the Press (the Ross Commission of 1947-9) attempted a more comprehensive explanation of news values. It found there were six categories of story then in common use:

Sport
News about people
Strange and amusing adventures
Tragedies and accidents
Crime
Public affairs.[2]

The Commission concluded:

"The idea of what constitutes news varies from [newspaper] office to office: a paper's standard of news values is one of the most distinctive facets of its personality. There are, however, certain elements common to all conceptions of news. To be news an event must first be interesting to the public, and the public for this purpose means for each paper the people who read the paper and others like them. Secondly, and most importantly, it must be new ..."[3]

This definition contains two important criteria: news must involve an element of change (it must be new), and it must be of interest to the audience. But like 'man bites dog' it begs a crucial question, in this case: what interests the public?

For reasons we will come to later (Chapter 4) the Ross Commission avoided digging too deeply into this central issue. So too have most subsequent commentators - with one notable exception.

In 1961 the *Guardian* newspaper set out its news priorities in a guide for new staff. The editor, Alastair Hetherington, later a research professor in media studies at Stirling University, listed seven factors likely to influence journalists in their news judgements:

Significance: social, economic, political, human
Drama: excitement, action and entertainment in the event
Surprise: freshness, newness, unpredictability
Personalities: royal, political, 'showbiz', others
Sex, scandal, crime
Numbers: scale of the event, number of people affected
Proximity: on our doorsteps, or 10,000 miles away [4]

Hetherington conceded that the concept of *Significance* needed further exploration, and later decided that in assessing the likely impact of a story journalists take into account the effect of the event on world peace and the prosperity, welfare and environment of the audience. Any change in the harmony of the status quo is regarded as important and potentially unwelcome news.[5] This insight is of crucial importance. For the first time there is a suggestion that there is a link between what the audience regards as news and its own security. As we will see later (Chapter 5) this definition of significance is fundamental to any explanation of, not just what news is, but *why* news is news.

The first systematic attempt to formulate the factors which make one story more newsworthy than others - comparative new evaluation - was carried out by two Swedish sociologists, Johan Galtung and Mari Ruge, in 1973.[6]

Basing their study on coverage of crises in the Congo, Cuba and Cyprus, Galtung and Ruge drew up a list of eight general conditions which have to be met before journalists consider an event to be news:

Frequency   The time span of the event relates to the frequency of the medium.   For instance radio news, which changes every hour, is more likely to be interested in a murder than long term trends.

Scale   The size of the story. Generally, the bigger the story the more likely it is to be reported. At the other end of the scale there is a threshold below which stories won't be reported at all.

Unambiguity   Events with rambling implications are less likely to be reported than those which are straightforward and clear cut.

Meaningfulness   An event is more likely to be reported if it accords with the cultural background of the journalist, or has implications for the journalist's home culture.

Consonance   Events which match the expectations and

pre-conceptions of the journalist will be given preference.

Unexpectedness   The more unpredictable, rare or unexpected the event, the more likely it is to be reported.

Continuity   Once an event has become news it will continue to be covered even if its scale is reduced.

Composition   A relatively insignificant story may be selected to balance a page or bulletin.

Galtung and Ruge went on to propose a further four criteria of importance to the western media:

Élite nations   There is a bias in favour of reporting events which happen in the first world. Stories from distant countries need to be stronger in absolute terms to achieve the same prominence.

Élite people   The ease with which an event passes the threshold of newsworthiness depends on the social status of the person involved. Relatively minor things which happen to someone in the public eye may be reported widely, whereas more significant events which happen to members of the public may well go unreported.

Personalisation   Events are seen as the actions of the individuals involved.

Negativity   Put simply, bad news is good news.

Galtung and Ruge's findings were pivotal. For the first time media analysts had a working tool with which to assess the comparative newsworthiness of stories. But their conclusions still don't constitute a complete definition of news. The two researchers failed to explain why their conditions affect the news value of stories, and while several of the factors on their list turn out to be relatively self-explanatory, the significance of others is obscure. For instance:

Why is bad news good news?
Why is the unexpected newsworthy?
Why are we fascinated by the trivial activities of the elite?

These important and unresolved questions suggest the existence of a hidden principle of news evaluation which escapes Galtung and Ruge's analysis.

To try and identify that underlying factor (or factors) we need to first separate off those conditions which are capable of a straightforward explanation. The best place to start is with the factors which stem from the mechanics of the news gathering process itself.

CHAPTER 2

OPERATIONAL AND STRUCTURAL FACTORS

A model of news values at least partially based on the operational constraints of the news gathering process is adopted by many media analysts. Other influences which need to be considered arise from both the structure of news organisations and the social and professional milieu of the newsroom.

Operational Factors

Four of Galtung and Ruge's conditions can be explained in purely operational terms: *frequency, unambiguity, continuity* and *composition*. To these must be added four conditions suggested by Alan Bell, a New Zealand journalist and socio-linguist, and two more put forward by Philip Schlesinger, a sociologist who spent seven years studying the operation of BBC newsrooms. Bell's additional factors are *competition, co-optation, prefabrication* and *predictability*.[7] Schlesinger emphasises the importance of *time constraints* and *logistics*.

Senior editors add that *financial constraints* also have an impact on their news judgement.

Time constraints, frequency and *unambiguity*

- Schlesinger describes radio as a 'stop watch' culture.[8] Journalists in radio, TV and daily papers work under much tighter time constraints than their colleagues in weekly papers and monthly magazines. In radio and TV bulletins are short, so the number of stories which can be included is limited. The deluge of press releases and other information which arrives on news desks therefore has to be pruned drastically. According to Schlesinger, BBC 'copy tasters' reject about ninety percent of incoming news agency copy. [9]

Pressure on air-time also means that the duration of a news story may prove critical. Even stories with a relatively high perceived news value may be cropped or dropped if a bulletin is running over length.

There is a bias in favour of covering simple, uncomplicated issues and events: all the relevant facts can be researched and collated quickly, and the story itself is capable of simple, clear and unambiguous interpretation. Precisely because such stories are self contained they have short lives. Journals or programmes with long 'lead times' (period before publication) prefer to concentrate on longer term issues and trends which won't date.

The earlier a story breaks before a newspaper's publication deadline, or before a bulletin goes on air, the more chance the editor has of arranging coverage.[10] If a story breaks after the deadline, its newsworthiness will depend on its shelf life. It may have lost its attraction or significance by the next time a publication opportunity comes round.

Logistics and Élite Nations

- The news gathering process involves deploying and subsequently controlling reporting staff, and in the case of the broadcast media, technical resources such as camera crews, outside broadcast vehicles and radio cars. News organisations have limited manpower and cover only those stories which they think are most newsworthy.[11]

The availability of technical facilities may determine whether or not a story is covered, and if so, in what depth. It's easier to report stories in urban centres than rural areas, and more feasible to arrange coverage in developed countries than it is in the third world, where communication links may be in short supply, antiquated or unreliable. This explains why élite nations are a favoured source of stories, though there is a further explanation which we will come to later (Chapter 5).

Financial Constraints

- Financial considerations may mean that staff simply aren't available for deployment. This will obviously restrict the number and type of stories covered.

Editors may come under pressure to select stories on the basis of cost rather than newsworthiness. Events with obvious significance and no awkward ramifications will be preferred to those which demand a heavy and extended commitment of staff and technical resources. Conversely, radio and television stations have to fill a set amount of air time, so financial stringency can affect the threshold at which a story is regarded as news. Faced with the need to cut costs, news editors will opt for cheaper material even if its news value might not normally merit transmission.

Composition

- Different media have different formats, established partly through precedent and partly through practical experience of what sells. Most formats are designed to offer the audience a balanced diet, so some items may be included purely to achieve variety.

Continuity

- Once a story is 'rolling' it has a proven news value, the background research has been done and the logistics have been planned and prepared. Journalists will therefore find it easier and more economical to continue coverage, rather than hunt around for another issue.

Competition

- In newspapers there is commercial pressure to get to a headline story first. This is a less direct pressure on the broadcast media, but in both cases the competitive element is important. A previously undiscovered story or part of a story can therefore achieve a higher news value than it might normally warrant. At the same time there is a 'me-too' factor which will lead journalists to endorse the news value attached to a scoop by a rival medium.

Co-optation

- A story which is only tangentially related can be interpreted and presented in terms of a high profile continuing story. For instance if a newspaper is running a major story, a connected though peripheral item with low intrinsic news value may be included in coverage.[12]

Prefabrication

- Many stories are written to a particular, if clichéd, format. In some cases the format may be imposed by law: journalists are greatly restricted in what they can and cannot say in the reporting of court cases, for example. Other stories may be prepared from press releases which render their content more attractive to the journalist because they are already couched in recognized 'news style'.

"A story which is marginal in news terms but written and available may be selected ahead of a much more newsworthy story which has to be researched and written from the ground up."[13]

Predictability

- An event is more likely to be covered if it has been prescheduled. This works in two ways. In a quiet provincial newsroom where interesting news material is in short supply, scheduled events form the backbone of the programme planning process. At the other end of the spectrum, busy national newsrooms rely on the 'diary' as a filter to short-list likely candidates from a wide range of available potential stories. It is also easier to plan logistics if a story has been prescheduled.

Predictability has strong links with *consonance* (see below): prescheduling of news can predetermine expectations of a story's news value.

Structural factors

The news value placed on events can be influenced by the structure of the news organisation, what Schlesinger refers to as 'evaluative baggage':

> "To put a construction on the news, impose a meaning on it, is inescapable, since the production process is one that at all stages involves the making of value judgements."[14]

Judgements are made against criteria defined by the cultural background of the journalist, the collective norms of the organisation and management policy directives.

As Schlesinger found in his study of BBC newsrooms, the predominant pressure in the BBC is to conform to a collective norm which is derived partly from historical precedent and partly from the common cultural background of the news-producers. Almost all BBC journalists support the broad goals of liberal parliamentary democracy and most are middle class graduates. This commonality of social background encourages a consensus view of the world which differs little from the corporate ideology: traditionally in the case of the BBC an assumed mission to report events impartially and without the overt imposition of value judgements, but with a covert bias towards a viewpoint determined by the norms of liberal parliamentary democracy and establishment middle class culture.

This consensus is self-reinforcing. For reasons we will come to   X later (Chapter 4) journalists write not for the audience but for themselves, their peers and their bosses.[15] Without external referents, value judgements made within such a highly inductive system tend to lean towards the collective norm.

The result of this can be journalistic 'tunnel vision', or *Consonance*: that is, an event which accords with the stereotypes or pre-conceptions of the journalist is more likely to register in the mind.   Consonance arises from 'media conventions' created and reinforced in the artificially closed world of the newsroom - though the reporter's own background and experience (or lack of it) may also have a part to play. Demonstrations are expected to be violent, company 'rationalisation' is assumed to involve job losses, and crime in certain areas may, often unfairly, be associated with specific ethnic groups.

Most British national newspapers adopt an overt political stance. In this case there may well be a distinction between a journalist's personal views and the corporate ideology, but the consensus dictates that these private views should not reflect themselves in the journalist's writing.

Changes in management policy will affect the value which is given to issues or events. In any large organisation the collective norm arrived at through precedent and mutual consent acquires a degree of inertia which tends to limit the impact of short term changes in management policy. However, the norm may have to alter if there is a major change in strategy. Such changes may be imposed to attract a bigger audience, or for political reasons. In the early nineteen eighties the American network CBS dramatically shifted ground towards a more tabloid approach to news in order to reach more viewers.[16] At the time of writing British ITV is considering doing the opposite, and moving upmarket in response to advertisers' demands that stations should attract a younger, more wealthy audience. The direction of the BBC's strategic policy is currently uncertain. Faced with the need to justify continued funding for the organisation's role as a public service broadcaster the Director General, John Birt, attempted to move the corporation towards the 'high ground', with an emphasis on news and current affairs coverage and analysis. But falling audience ratings have now apparently forced a U-turn, and in July 1993 the Controller of BBC1 Alan Yentob announced plans to once again service the needs of a wider mass audience.

"Management can oscillate between strategies of entertaining and informing, depending on how they perceive the demands of the consumer of news programmes ... the hunt for consumer loyalty is related both to short term success and long term survival."[17]

14

CHAPTER 3

SOCIO-POLITICAL FACTORS

No news organisation is an island. Apart from operational
constraints and internal structural influences, the news value
given to an event and its interpretation can also be affected by
external pressures exerted by governments, pressure groups
and the society within which the news organisation is
embedded.

News is a powerful social and political force, shaping the way
the audience sees the world. Both ruling élites and opposition
pressure groups therefore attach great importance to controlling
or at least influencing the media, either to reinforce their
position or to help legitimise their cause.

In some cases such control is direct, complete and overt. The
media broadcast and publish stories which bolster the norms
imposed by the ruling élite. The result is propaganda: the
choice of news stories is determined by what the establishment

wants the audience to know and how it wants people to think.

In most countries with a liberal democratic tradition, the media operates independently of state control, exercising a freedom to observe the internal norms of the organisation - though these norms often accord with a self-generated consensus which itself sits comfortably within the wider norms of the society the news organisation serves.

This is not to say that attempts at more direct control aren't made. If the ruling élite feels threatened, it may attempt to directly influence the selection of news items and the slant placed on them. Prior to 1979, Labour leaders in Britain criticised the BBC for anti-Labour bias. Following the accession of Margaret Thatcher, the corporation was frequently accused of anti-Conservative bias. Such attacks become more strident before elections: criticism was particularly virulent in the run-up to the 1992 election, a contest the Conservatives were not sure they would win. At times like this the need for political survival will often induce ruling élites to deliberately confuse the national interest and the interests of the government or even individual ministers.

The perceived need to control the media grows in wartime, or when counter insurgency measures are in force. Attempts at control may take the form of news management, which was used by the British and Americans during the Falkland and Gulf Wars. The information released to journalists is carefully chosen by the military authorities, and the journalists themselves are encouraged to see their role as part of the war effort. Journalists who adopt the establishment consensus that the national interest is paramount are regarded as acceptable -

they effectively become 'self-censoring'.[18] Alternatively, if the authorities fear a situation may be unmanageable in media terms, they may simply impose a straightforward clamp-down on news, or 'news blackout', a policy adopted by the United States during the American invasion of Grenada in 1983.[19]

Whether news organisations accede to outside control depends on the degree to which they endorse the establishment position, and also their own vulnerability to censure. The BBC has crossed swords with successive governments on a variety of issues, mostly involving national security and the role of the security services, especially in Northern Ireland. While the government has indirect but real control over the legitimacy of its source of income - the licence fee - the corporation knows it must tread warily.

External pressures may not always come from the 'establishment'. In a pluralistic society many different power groups lobby for media attention at some stage:

> "The State, the law, their competitors, their audiences, and (not least) the people on whose activities they report all constrain the choices open to journalists and broadcasters."[20]

This conflict of interest is most influential when it occurs within the news organisation itself:

> "The corporations and capitalists who own the means of news production can mount campaigns, of exposure and investigation, or of war-mongering and witch-hunts, which help to alter the political or social direction of a

17

country. Clearly such power leads to a dangerous imbalance between those that control that power and the rest of us. The news, inevitably, is what they say it is."[21]

The effect of these socio-political influences can be traced through choice of stories, the significance given to them and the choice of words and pictures used, or omitted, in their compilation. Just how this process works is the subject of *Semiotics*, the study of the social production and communication of meaning.

The Language of News

Several commentators argue that news values are determined by the expression of socio-political influences through linguistic constructs. In his book *Understanding News* John Hartley insists that:

"... news values are neither natural nor neutral. They form a code which sees the world in a very particular way ... [they] are in fact an ideological code..."[22]

In order to appreciate how our perceptions of events and issues can be moulded by language, we need to understand something of the ephemeral complexities of the labyrinth of meaning which lurks behind the obvious value of words.

To communicate concepts we use *Signs*. A sign is made up of two parts, the Signifier and the Signified. For example, the word 'dog' means, in English, a four legged animal with certain specific characteristics which we associate with dogs. The signifier is the arbitrary symbol ('dog') we use to denote

18

the concept itself: the signified (the animal).

Signs in turn are built into *Codes*, conventions of usage which have particular values according to the social group, and the context, in which they're applied. So signs can connote different things. For instance, depending on the social idiom, 'dog' can also mean 'rough, unkempt', or, again, 'randy'. The accepted connotation of a word can also change over time. Take the word 'gay'. In 1960 the *Pocket Oxford Dictionary* defined 'gay' as 'light-hearted, mirthful and brilliant'. Over the last thirty years this signifier has acquired a quite different, although obviously not unrelated, usage. What Hartley calls the 'multi-accentuality' of signs allows us to alter the connotations of a sign, providing it is done with general consent. This implies that the meaning of a word is not absolute. A word in fact only means what we all agree it should mean. Meaning is:

> "... strictly a social phenomenon [which] tends to be multiplied up from the particular sign or interactive utterance, until a single sign can be loaded with multiple meanings going far beyond what it seems actually to 'say'."[23]

The relevance of this relativity of meaning to news values is that both journalist and audience can be driven to ascribe values to a situation that are derived from the 'news codes' with which journalist and audience are both familiar. For instance, an English radio presenter could choose interview 'clips' which describe an IRA bombing as: "courageous, daring, and effective"; however, the audience would be deeply confused because what they would regard as the conventional code system was not being used. They would expect to hear what Hartley calls 'boo' words like "outrage, cowardly and ineffectual."

Persistent use of a code in a particular way can override the audience's preferred reading, a technique which is frequently used by politicians and other pressure groups. For instance, if the word is not obviously being used in a health care context, 'drugs' can connote 'law-breaker, anarchy, crime, wild youth'. The word becomes a *Myth*. As Hartley explains:

> "... myths are produced when signs are multiplied up so that their 'denotative' meaning includes (apparently intrinsically) signs of conceptual values."[24]

A number of such loaded signs, when presented together, can present a 'connotative curtain' which makes it difficult to sort out the unloaded meaning of the words and the concepts they would otherwise denote.

To illustrate how this works in practice, consider the following example. A BBC regional TV reporter was sent to cover a legal 'rave' in East Anglia. The police turned up in force, strip searched many youngsters and claimed a massive drugs haul, which they then argued as adequate justification for their tactics. The reporter wanted to balance the police view by highlighting the strip searching and apparent over-policing of an event which he judged to be legal, relatively well-regulated and didn't constitute a threat to law and order. In a live interview which immediately followed the journalist's report a senior police spokesman strongly defended his position, repeatedly using the words 'drugs', 'young people', and 'rave'.

He was thereby able to create a connotative curtain which was intended to sway audience opinion in his favour through persistent use of myth words associated with lawlessness, dissent and a threat to society. The emphasis, and therefore the news value of the story, was changed by manipulation of the mechanics of language.

While valuable as an aid to interpreting and explaining the way news values are determined by the perceptions of the journalist and the audience, a semiotic model of news values is not exhaustive. It doesn't explain the remainder of Galtung and Ruge's conditions. And while it gives us an insight into the way in which journalists and audience communicate, like the other models we have looked at so far the socio-linguistic approach to news analysis ignores the possibility that other factors may determine the audience's perception of news, regardless of outside influence.

CHAPTER 4

THE MISSING LINK

The way the news-gathering operation works, the cultural background of the journalists, outside political and social forces and even the structure of language itself can all determine which stories are used and the way the details of the stories are interpreted and presented. These factors are important, but they don't offer a complete definition of news. For a start they leave seven of Galtung and Ruge's conditions for news unexplained:

Why should the unexpected be newsworthy?
Why is bad news 'good news'?
Why is the size of an event relevant?
Why are audiences parochial in their interests?
Why are we fascinated by famous people?
Why are interested in the affairs of élite nations?
Why are we more interested in people than things?

Media analysts themselves admit the picture given by currently models of news is incomplete:

"Achieving relevance for a story causes much head scratching in newsrooms."[25]

"It is a true platitude that news is bad, although it is a difficult question why the negative makes news".[26]

The problem is that the conventional models of news we have been examining share a fundamental limitation. They concentrate on factors which decide what news values are imposed on the audience.

In the operational model physical factors, such as limitations on time and resources affect the choice of story.

The structural model argues that the structure of the news organisation itself - its traditions and the consensual attitudes of staff - determines the journalist's news judgement.

In both these models the imposition of news values on the audience is a by-product of the news process.

The socio-political model suggests that news values are imposed on the audience deliberately. News organisation proprietors, advertisers, politicians and commercial interests may attempt to put pressure on the news gathering process, affecting both the choice of stories and the way they are written.

None of these models address the simple question: what does the audience perceive as news?

This indifference is not surprising. The mass media represent a mass audience: a heterogeneous amalgam of thousands, even millions, of different individuals who have as many different needs, aspirations and opinions. While audience surveys can give a generalised 'audience profile', most news producers are convinced that members of the audience can never be catered for, or treated, as individuals. As Schlesinger puts it:

"The 'total' audience remains an abstraction, made real on occasion by letters or telephone calls, encounters of a random kind in public places, or perhaps more structured ones such as conversations with liftmen, barmen and taxi drivers."[27]

A number of commentators conclude that mass communicators have only the haziest concept of the people that make up their audience, and "are not just ignorant of the nature of their audience, they are uninterested."[28]

It is not only broadcasters who adopt what Hartley calls an: "Olympian view of the audience as a large mass of undifferentiated individuals"[29]. Gans quotes a top American magazine editor:

"If we had to think about how our readers feel, all twenty million of them, we'd freeze." [30]

24

Faced with the apparent impossibility of judging the needs and opinions of the audience, journalists claim only to write for themselves, their peers, their sources, their editors and even their families[31]. Schlesinger quotes typical comments from BBC news staff:

"I'm really only writing for myself and my wife."

"I can only take what goes on in my own home as an indicator of interest." [32]

This pessimism is shared by most media analysts. Schlesinger refers to a 'structural lacuna' between the producers and consumers of news. A leading proponent of the operational and structural models of news evaluation, he argues that:

"... broadcast news is the outcome of standardised production routines; these routines work themselves out within an organisational structure which has no adequate point of contact with the audience ... there is, therefore, no sense in which one can talk of a communication taking place which is truly alive to the needs of the news audience." [33]

The inevitable danger of this gulf between journalist and audience is alienation. If the listener, viewer or reader finds little relevance in the message, they will switch off. Worse, they will absorb a garbled understanding of the story. Research quoted by Bell indicates audience recall of broadcast news rarely exceeds thirty percent, and can fall as low as five percent. [34] If that percentage is to be improved, the gulf between audience and journalist must be bridged. We must tackle head-on the crucial question which the Ross Commission and most other commentators have side-stepped:

What sort of stories interest the public?

CHAPTER 5

AN ANTHROPOLOGICAL MODEL

As we have seen, journalists and analysts agree that tailoring news to the needs and interests of a mass audience is an impossible task. But if we could establish a factor which determines the interest of every individual within a mass audience, we would then for the first time be able to define what *the audience* regards as news. By extension, it would also be possible to derive a working model of news evaluation which would allow the journalist to select, write and order stories in such a way as to maximise its impact on that audience.

To do this we need to pose the right question. We need to ask, not "What interests people?", but "What motivates people's interest?".

For a start we can discount specific subjects like train spotting, making wine or driving fast cars. These are minority interests.

The more primitive drives of sex, food or greed are universal, as all of us at some time are hungry, or acquisitive, or feel lust. But unless we are obsessive, even these powerful motivations do not dominate our lives all the time. They do however point towards a factor which does.

Sex, food and greed are all relevant to *survival*. And the one thing which interests all of the people all of the time is their own security.

In fact, as American psychologist Robert Franken explains, our interest in change which may affect our physical security is deep rooted and instinctive. When faced with a threat, our bodies automatically make the necessary arrangements for fight or flight: the heart rate increases, the liver releases glucose for energy and the spleen releases more blood corpuscles to improve the flow of oxygen to the muscles. We become intensely alert as the brain evaluates the various options:

> "Whenever we interpret an event as threatening ... we are likely to experience an increase in arousal, both cortical and autonomic ... it is important that the body be prepared to deal with that threat, both mentally and physically."[35]

The importance we attach to threats to our own security and well-being accords with Hetherington's observation:

> "... in estimating significance most journalists in national newspapers or broadcasting are concerned with events and

decisions which may affect the world's peace, the prosperity or welfare of people in Britain and abroad, and the environment in which we live."[36]

However, it could well be argued that most of the events, decisions and personalities featured in the news do not threaten our own physical security. Many stories relate to events which don't directly affect us, or to individuals whose lives and deeds are most unlikely to impinge directly on our own. These are 'social' stories, and to suggest that we are motivated to show interest in events which are peripheral to our own security concerns requires the hypothesis that we are as deeply and primitively committed to our social security as we are to our physical well-being.

Interestingly, just such a hypothesis exists. It was developed by anthropologists to explain the development of human intelligence, but as we will see it also turns out to be crucial to an understanding of what motivates audience interest in news.

The Machiavellian hypothesis

Traditional theories about human social evolution stress the key role of technical innovation in the development of intelligence. When the immediate forerunners of man made the transition from a foraging forest lifestyle to that of savannah hunter, they were forced to walk upright. To hunt, to flee from the specialised predators with which they were now in competition, these primates needed to see over obstacles, and they had to have speed. The resulting development of an upright, bi-pedal gait had a useful spin-off: it freed the fore-limbs to make and manipulate tools and weapons. Anthropologists concluded that

29

this ability to make and use tools created a technical intelligence which then fed back into the development of language and a more complex group social structure which was better suited to survival.[37]

Since 1976 a number of anthropologists and psychologists have challenged this hypothesis. They argue that a primate (ape or man) doesn't need intellect to make and use simple tools, any more than a Blue Tit should be regarded as intelligent because it opens milk bottle tops. The skills can be learned by trial and error. But intelligence is needed to cope with the complexities of the social environment in which those technical skills are learned! [38]

Living within a close knit social group places peculiar demands on the individual. There is a need to co-operate, but also to compete over the selection of mates, food resources, allies, grooming partners and position in the hierarchy. [39] In order to maintain its own position within this complex social milieu, the individual is under strong selective pressure to develop an understanding of causality and the notion of reciprocity. [40]

There is clear evidence of this social intelligence in non-human primates. Apes and monkeys with no technical aptitude have shown they are capable of planning and thinking through the consequences of highly complex social exchanges. Chimpanzees in particular demonstrate a high degree of deceit and manipulation of others in pursuit of their own ends. In fact, so intelligent and complex is their duplicity that close parallels have been drawn between non-human primate politics and the principles of human government described by the 16th century political observer Nicolo Machiavelli.[41]

This new insight into primate behaviour led to the 'Machiavellian intelligence hypothesis', which proposes that intelligence evolved not for the benefit of the group, or because of the use of tools, but to help the individual gain a position of social advantage within the group.

According to this hypothesis, society can be seen as a bubbling percolation of individual aspirations which may or may not have beneficial implications for the group as a whole. Dr Phyllis Lee, a biological anthropologist at the University of Cambridge, explains:

"From a primate perspective the group is a series of individuals with individual needs which are best met within the context of a co-operative, as well as conflicting, group. There is a constant need to reconcile this desire to cooperate within the group with the need for individual attainment of resources. The group is merely the outcome of that co-operation and conflict... In a social group we're forced to solve uncertainty problems within a social construct, so we need to cope with the complex burden of sociality."

The Machiavellian hypothesis suggests a far more dynamic view of primate social interaction than that offered by the traditional model. Above all it implies a double survival pressure on the individual. Not only are there risks in the physical environment: predators, availability of food sources and so on. There are also uncertainties in the social environment which select for the individual's chances of survival.

By definition uncertainties involve change.

Coping With Uncertainty

There are two fundamental ways of dealing with uncertainty in a survival situation.

The first is to be aware of the possibility of change and monitor for it. This pressure selects for an inbuilt curiosity which allows both the detection and evaluation of novelty in the environment. Primates, including man, are 'neotenous' - that is, they retain into adulthood certain characteristics of infancy which have a survival benefit. The aspect of neoteny which concerns us most here is this: primates never lose the curiosity which is characteristic only of the young in many other species. Lambs are quick-witted, playful and intensely inquisitive, but these traits disappear almost entirely by the time lambs become sheep. Primates, on the other hand, are forced by the eternal uncertainty of their physical and social environments to be on the look out for change, and to learn from mistakes:

"For primates, the most important thing is monitoring novelty for environmental risk. [An awareness of] novelty is part of understanding the uncertainty of the social and physical environment. Generation of cognitive processes around the understanding of novelty is important, because it allows the individual to assess its position, and that's crucial not only to its personal survival but the survival of its genes. Novelty, whether natural or social pushes learning forward, creating an opportunity to construct hypotheses about the world.." (Lee)

The second defence against uncertainty is the ability to model situations in time. In other words to think ahead, predicting the outcome of actions and interactions before they occur.

The Role of Communication

The ability to model the outcome of a course of action has little use if the model isn't applied, either in a co-operative mode for the protection of the group, or during social conflict to gain advantage for the individual. This generates a selection pressure for some means of communicating not just information, but also complicated temporal models incorporating predictive concepts. It is this function which distinguishes language as we know it from the simple warning calls used by most animals subject to environmental uncertainty.

In order for communication to take place, two conditions are required. The communicator must attract the attention of the communicatee, and more crucially, the communicatee must be disposed to receive that communication. Given the selection pressure for communication, we can infer that humans have developed an in-built predisposition to communicate and receive both information and cognitive constructs in order to boost their chances of both physical and social survival.

Towards a Definition of News

If current thinking on the evolution of intelligence is correct, we can sum up its significance for our purposes in the following terms:

People are fundamentally predisposed to awareness of change in their physical and social environment, and to build and communicate cognitive constructs which will negotiate an improvement in the individual's chances of survival.

This position is extremely important. From it we can deduce the fundamental factors which motivate attentiveness in an audience. They are:

- a fascination with *Change*, both physical and social.

- a need to know how that change will affect the individual. We can call this *Security Concern*.

Change

Without change, information cannot be interpreted as news. Change is important because it involves uncertainty, which in turn generates attention and concern. 'Man bites dog' is news because its unexpected.

The degree of concern created is in direct proportion to the degree to which the status quo is likely to be altered. If minor repairs are carried out to Big Ben, this will be relevant to no-one outside the works department at Westminster. If on the other hand the clock tower is to be demolished, there is a radical degree of change and the news value of the story is enhanced accordingly.

This example highlights another significance of change. Fear of uncertainty creates a need for what Aaron Katcher of the University of Pennsylvania calls 'icons of constancy'[42]: symbols of continuity which reassure the audience that change will be controlled and its potentially harmful effects minimised. In time, familiar institutions, objects, landmarks and even individuals acquire an 'iconic momentum'. Change is interpreted by the audience not only as an attack on its physical security, but as a threat to the psychological bulwarks it has created against change itself.

Inherent in the notion of change is topicality. Change has to be happening now or threatened for the future to carry a security threat. If the event happened in the past, it's not news but history. However, because they're 'safe' in this sense, historical events and their interpretation also acquire the status of icons of constancy. Traditions accumulate their own iconic momentum, and become vulnerable to the intrinsic iconoclasm of change. Consequently, stories which involve unexpected reinterpretation of the past carry a high news value.

The *rate* of change is important. Slow change gives people time to adjust to uncertainty; the more rapid and dramatic the alteration in the status quo, the more impact the story will have. A strong story which is in the news for a considerable time may start to lose the interest of the audience unless some radical element of change can be introduced. Such news fatigue is noticeable during long drawn out conflicts. If the nature of the conflict is not clear cut, and there is no resolution to the fighting in sight, its 'product life' as a story will be limited and media attention will start to shift away to some other issue.

Controversy is a key element in news. It generates uncertainty, and implies potential change. Journalists will often go out of their way to highlight the element of controversy in a story simply because it implicitly suggests either an unwelcome change to the status quo, or a threat to a previously secure icon of constancy.

Change can be engineered. Journalists will often inject new life into an old story by highlighting some artificially imposed element of change: for instance, an anniversary. Another favourite application of engineered change is to give undue emphasis to an element of uncertainty in order to artificially embellish the newsworthiness of the story. An otherwise unpromising story is made newsworthy by isolating an element of potential change, boosting its apparent importance through selective use of facts or quotation, and then contriving to resolve the uncertainty by putting the story back into its real context. For instance, a factory might announce future plans to reorganise its operation. In reality, these plans may not involve redundancies, but by dwelling on the possibility of lay-offs the journalist will be able to extract dark warnings of industrial disruption from the unions, and counter-balance these with increasingly futile-sounding denials from management. When the journalist has grown tired of the sport, or a more interesting story comes along, the original management statement is highlighted and the potential threat of change reduced to its proper level of significance. This is a technique called 'setting the story up to knock it down', and is widely used by journalists to enhance the apparent news value of a story.

Returning to Galtung and Ruge's conditions for news, the importance of change as a basic factor in news evaluation explains why *Unexpectedness* is a condition for news.

It also explains *Negativity*, why 'bad news is good news'. All change creates uncertainty. If the negative implications are obvious then change is that much more likely to attract the audience's attention. It is in the individual's interest to monitor developments closely, to evaluate the security implications of the change and to assess what action to take: fight, flight or social negotiation. In general, good news is of less interest than bad news because there is less to worry about, and therefore there is no need to plan avoiding action.

Our instinctive urge to be inquisitive about change is so strong that change itself can have a news value, even though the change concerned can have no implications for our security. This sort of story includes the light, often humorous items which are known in the broadcasting industry as "And finally's..." because they usually appear last in the bulletin. A memorable example some years ago featured a duck which had been taught to ride a skate-board; another involved hard-bitten fire-fighters giving oxygen to a family of baby mice which had been caught in a field fire. Research shows that this type of item is often recalled best by the audience.[43]

Security Concern

Humans share with all animals two fundamental concerns and they both relate to survival: survival of self, and genetic survival. These are deep seated drives which colour, consciously or unconsciously, the way we relate to each other and the world around us. As Hetherington puts it:

" ... anything which threatens people's peace, prosperity and well being is news and likely to make headlines" [44]

The threat can either be physical and environmental, or it may arise from social pressures. Bell observes:

"Conflict between people, political parties or nations is a staple of news." [45]

Hartley agrees:

"The bread and butter of news is conflict, violence, rivalry, and disagreement" [46]

According to the Machiavellian hypothesis social groups are much more than static collections of individuals who have bonded together for mutual self-protection. Instead society can be seen as an ever-shifting matrix of relationships formed by individuals as they reconcile the relative advantages of conflict and co-operation as the best means for attaining resources.

As we have seen, in order to achieve that reconciliation individuals need information: to negotiate their own position within a constantly changing interplay of relationships people need to know not only what's going on, but also the relative strengths and weaknesses of other members of the social group. In practice this means we are under strong selective pressure to keep abreast of the shifting patterns of social interactions in society. In particular there is a need to monitor the behaviour of élite groups, as their behaviour is most likely to have an effect on our security.

Boundaries of Relevance

The strength of this drive to monitor for change depends not only on the likely relevance of the threat, but the relationship to us of the individual or group affected.

In order of priority, our first concern is for ourselves. Our second interest is the survival of our genes: in other words, our immediate family group. Thirdly, we are concerned for the security of our immediate friends and relations: individuals can strengthen their negotiating position within society by forming a sub-group which is founded on mutual empathy, or in a more crudely genetic sense, on the wider family unit. Finally, there is a concern for the integrity of the community as a whole. Beyond that we draw a *boundary of relevance*, the limits of which are determined by our ability to understand and model our relational links with others, and therefore their relevance to our own security concerns. (See Figure 1, overleaf.) As Hartley puts it, citing Berger and Luckmann:

"This domain is the realm of 'reality maintenance', where primary socialisation takes place. It promotes a 'subjective reality' which organises and confirms our consciousness of ourselves, and our (more or less successful) habit of assuming a central place for our consciousness, with the world outside receding in circles of ever decreasing relevance." [47]

Figure 1: Boundary of Relevance

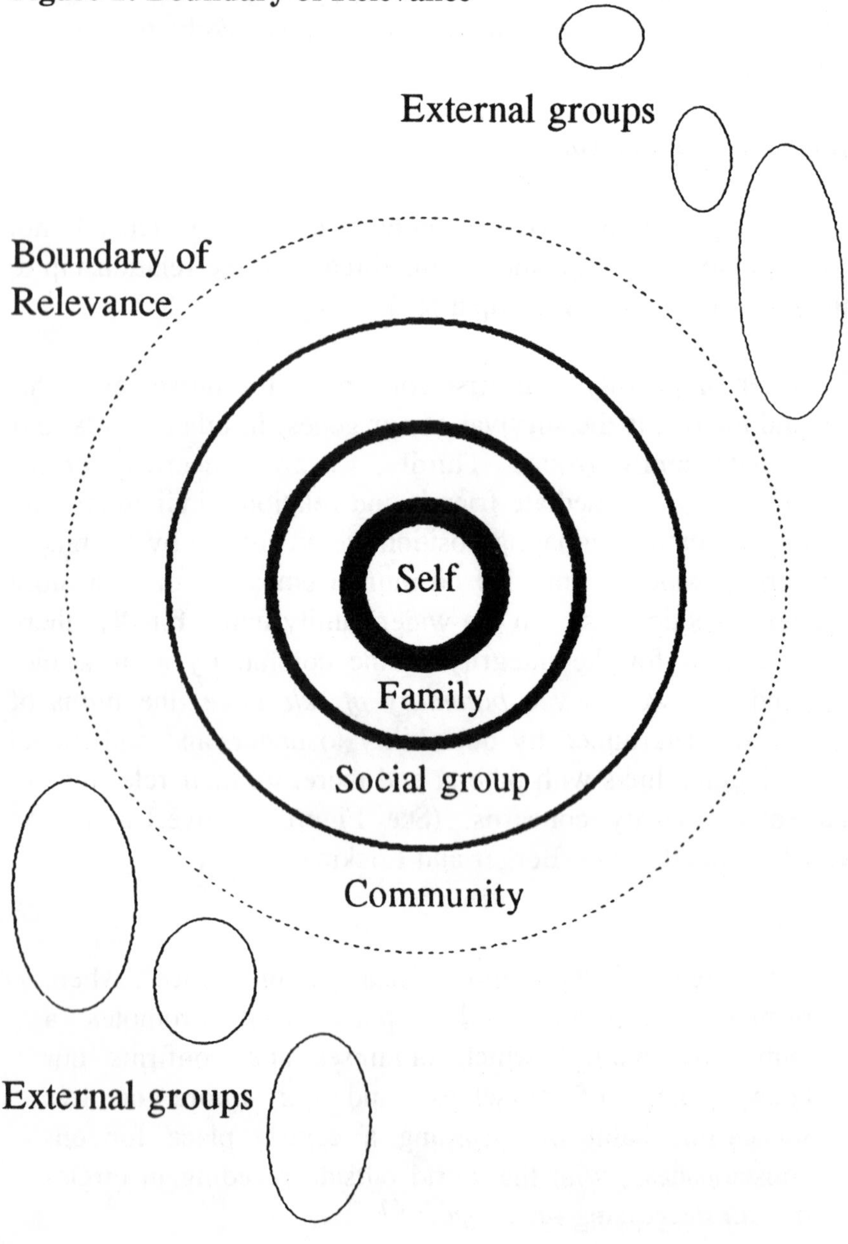

External groups

Boundary of
Relevance

Self

Family

Social group

Community

External groups

The factor which determines the position of this boundary of relevance is the ability to understand and model the behaviour of the external social group with reference to ourselves. (Figure 2) Members of closed (or xenophobic) cultures impose the boundary not far beyond the social or even family group. In parts of New Guinea, for example, tribes in neighbouring valleys are culturally distinct from each other. At the other extreme, in some societies - or at least in certain sections of those societies - cultural affiliations can be pan-global. The community in this case is much larger, with diffuse boundaries.

Figure 2: External group outside boundary

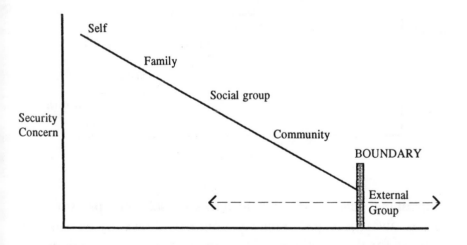

If a social group can identify common ground with a group outside its boundary of relevance it may choose to adopt the external group as an 'affiliated community', bringing the culture or group within its area of interest. Or to put it another way, the concept of community is flexible, and can be extended or contracted to include or exclude external groups. In broad terms, a sense of commonality, whether based on culture, religion or simple humanity, will create an empathy which may encourage one group to extend at least peripheral security concern to another (Figure 3):

Figure 3: External group absorbed inside boundary

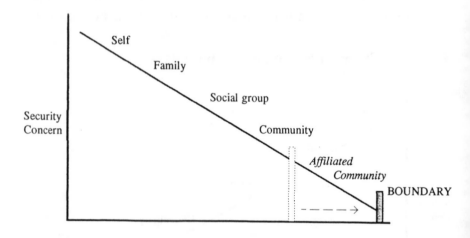

Explaining news evaluation in terms of selective pressure for social awareness and security concern allows us to suggest reasons for the remainder of Galtung and Ruge's conditions for news:

Scale

- The bigger the event the more significance it is likely to have for our security, either negative or positive.

Personalisation

- It follows from the significance the audience attaches to social factors that complex policies and issues can best be assimilated in terms of the human element. An audience will relate better to an event if it is couched in terms of the personalities involved.

Meaningfulness and Élite nations

- As we have seen (Chapter 2), meaningfulness is partly an operational condition determined by the logistics of extracting news from a particular area: élite nations have better communications with the outside world. Élite nations are also generally more familiar to us, either because of common ethnic or cultural links, or, in some cases, because of frequent exposure of their cultures in films and other mass media. The more dissimilar a culture, the less likely it is that its activities will be of interest to the audience. Journalists are motivated by the same mind-set:

> "News is [seen as] what happens to one Englishman, ten Germans or a thousand Indians." [48]

The news value of events beyond the boundary of relevance of the audience can be enhanced in the short term by relating their significance to the security concerns of the audience. For example, the newsworthiness of the demise of the rain forests is strengthened by signposting the implications for 'our' climate. In the longer term, explanatory and persistent coverage by the media may encourage the audience to bring the object of the story itself within its boundary of relevance. For instance, famine in Africa will have little impact on an audience which has no knowledge of the society or culture affected. Regular media coverage which stresses the human element of the problem, as well as explaining its background, will forge empathic bridges with the audience, encouraging support for charity or relief efforts. From the journalist's point of view it will also generate spontaneous interest in news coverage: the audience will have accepted the famine victims as an affiliated community.

Alternatively, boundaries of relevance can be used to 'fence off' an audience from a community. In his disturbing portrayal of the influence of power politics on the management of news, *Distant Voices*, the journalist John Pilger argues that in time of war, the 'enemy' community is deliberately dehumanised by the establishment, and co-operative sections of the media, in order to ensure that military action is not compromised by ethical or humanitarian qualms. Individuals are presented as 'stick men', aliens without depth or personality, with whom the audience can find and feel little commonality. The identity of the community as a whole is subsumed within a caricature of its leaders, which can be vilified, ridiculed or otherwise manipulated for propaganda purposes: the German nation becomes 'Hitler'; the Iraquis, 'Saddam Hussein'. Actions which in any other context would be regarded as atrocities are legitimised by a process of 'normalisation': the dead become statistics, civilian casualties are swept under the carpet as 'collateral damage', and military strikes have no more human relevance than a game of 'space invaders':

"Normalising can only be successful *once distance has been established* [my italics]. General Schwarzkopf's video game show during the Gulf War, which television dutifully transmitted at peak times, was an outstanding example of this. Like the pilots who dropped the 'smart bombs', politicians, journalists, bureaucrats and the public, all of us, were kept at a distance."[49]

Power élites and *Élite nations*

- According to Phyllis Lee, studies of non-human primates reveal:

"... the incredible social attraction of high rank. Individuals compete with each other within groups to have access to others with high rank. Even though there may be no return, it may help them to acquire higher status themselves."

We are interested in the activities and affairs of power élites and élite nations for two reasons: first, they are in a position to directly influence our physical security; secondly, monitoring 'who's doing what to whom' puts us in a better position to re-negotiate our own social position.

Non-power Élites

- While awareness of the behaviour of power élites has an obvious benefit in terms of survival advantage, it doesn't explain fascination with non-power élites: artists, pop stars, film stars, and the Royal Family.

In his study of attitudes to the British monarchy, *Talking of the Royal Family*, Michael Billig concludes that the royals are effectively icons of constancy. In a changing world they represent a bulwark against uncertainty, a security blanket to cling to in a world bereft of political, social and religious bench-marks:

"... the past heritage of royalty - or, the imagining of its historical continuity - offers a promise for the future which might otherwise be a disconcerting blank. 'Our' lives will run in parallel to 'theirs' and the continuity will be reassuringly shared. Overwhelming transience and obsolescence seem to be held in check, while a touch of royalty dignifies the present as the heritage for the future."[50]

Many journalists dismiss popular enthusiasm for royalty as a tabloid driven phenomenon. Billig's interpretation would suggest that in fact this interest is simply the individual's way of monitoring the stability of society - its customs and its mores - as a whole.

It follows that anything which affects the continuity of the Royal Family threatens the security of those who regard them as icons. This threat in turn generates an overwhelming desire for information, a factor which was exploited by tabloid press coverage of stories about the sex lives of the Prince and the Princess of Wales in 1992/3 - the so-called 'Squidgy Tape' and 'Camilla-gate' scandals.

The potency of this need for a 'guarantor of stability' is demonstrated by the fact that cultures will co-opt icons of constancy if they don't possess suitable candidates of their own. Dr Ray Abrahams, a Cambridge social anthropologist, cites the obsessive interest shown by Finnish villagers in the marriage of the Prince and Princess and Wales in 1981.

The social importance of pop stars, football players, actors and others can also be explained in terms of iconic status. But we should not ignore the importance of the 'role model'. Particularly for disadvantaged sections of the community, successful members of those sections can provide an 'ambition channel' which demonstrates to their peers how they too can aspire to social position and rank; alternatively, they provide a cathartic focus for those whose ambitions are likely to remain unrealised.

The Machiavellian hypothesis offers a possible additional explanation for the attraction of non-power élite groups and individuals.

In order to assess our own position in a complex social hierarchy, we rely on indicators which 'flag' the social status of others. Power élites are characterised by the attention, adulation and respect they receive from other members of society, as well as a disproportionate allocation of wealth or physical resources. It is possible that when these social indicators are conferred on an individual not in the power élite, they trigger a 'power élite response' in society members.

The Machiavellian hypothesis also suggests reasons for the newsworthiness of two very different sources of stories: disasters and animals.

Disasters

- Accidents and disasters have a hypnotic attraction for the public and always make big news. But what is the appeal of events in which the audience is not directly involved? There are three possible explanations.

The first is that fascination with disaster is altruistic: people want to help. The argument against this is the motorway crash syndrome. People slow down and even obstruct police and ambulance crews just to glimpse what's happening.

The second model argues that public fascination with the disaster stems from voyeurism. Proponents suggest that we get a cosy glow, even a vicarious excitement watching radical and damaging change affect other people.

The Machiavellian hypothesis implies the 'appeal' of a disaster would seem to lie, firstly, in its primary security concern, the desire to analyse a risk situation to see whether there are lessons to be learned. Secondly, there is an unconscious need to assess the situation in terms of social change, to monitor the misfortune of others in terms of the enhanced survival possibilities this may offer to the unharmed observer.

Animals

- Animal stories are guaranteed an audience in those cultures in which animals have social relevance and are not just regarded as prey or food.

James Serpell, director of the Companion Animal Research

Group at the University of Cambridge suggests three reasons for public interest which accord with a Machiavellian model of human behavioural motivation.

The first is fear. Large or dangerous animals inspire primary security concern.

Secondly, some animals have physical features which trigger a protective response in humans because of their similarity to babies: big eyes, disproportionately large head for body size and non-threatening behaviour. This so-called 'pædomorphism' explains why pandas and koalas make 'good copy'. A strong and instinctive urge to concern ourselves with the security of our own young back-fires, causing us to bring inside our boundary of relevance animals which are in reality anti-social and unempathic.

Thirdly, pets function as icons of constancy, offering unquestioning devotion and ego reinforcement which may not be available to the owner from other humans. It is interesting to speculate that, in terms of the Machiavellian hypothesis, the appeal of companion animals may be enhanced precisely because they offer a reliable and sympathetic social bond which requires no social negotiation.

Conclusion

An anthropological approach to the analysis of news values satisfactorily accounts for previously unexplained conditions for newsworthiness set by other commentators. It also establishes those factors which motivate audience interest in news:

The primary news value of an event depends on the degree of change from the status quo, and individuals' perception of the implications of that change for the physical, environmental, psychological and social security of themselves, their families and their community in decreasing order of priority.

The practical constraints of the news gathering process, the collective norms of the journalists, the desire of power élites to manipulate the public and the structure of language can all affect what goes into the news and how it is interpreted. But the influence of these secondary factors can only be measured by their impact on the audience, and that will be determined by the primary factors of change and security concern.

CHAPTER 6

WORKING WITH NEWS VALUES

Theories about why and how news works can only really be tested in the newsroom. If a model is applied to story selection, news writing and presentation, and is found to tally with reality, then we can say it has a relevance. If it can also be used to maximise the impact of the story on the audience, then it has a practical value as well. Applying the anthropological hypothesis allows us to do just that, precisely because the model defines what elements in a story will generate audience interest.

Story Selection

TV and radio bulletins are short, and the number of potential stories virtually limitless. It is, therefore, necessary to select those items which are most likely to attract the attention of the audience.

By assessing the change involved in each story, and the implications of that change for the audience, the journalist can assess their relative news value. But before we can do so, we first need to establish certain basic parameters. We need to decide the type of station or newspaper we are working for, the geographical location of the audience, and the general characteristics of the audience.

Clearly the type of stories which interest people will vary as to whether it is a local or national audience. A new treatment for baldness will be of interest to bald people everywhere. A minor story of local significance may feature prominently in a local paper, but will be of no interest whatsoever to a national paper.

It follows that the geographical location of the audience is important. The fact that a Colchester company has created a hundred jobs will be of greater interest in Colchester than it will in, say, Inverness. Equally the state of the Icelandic fish harvest will hold little interest for an audience in the centre of England.

Assessing the general characteristics of the target audience means simply knowing in the broadest terms which groups we are addressing. For instance, is the audience urban or rural? Is it a predominantly white, middle class audience, or are there large and clearly defined ethnic minority groups? For the purposes of the following exercise we will assume we are working for a local radio station in the east of East of England with a predominantly small-scale urban audience and a broadly homogeneous population of Anglo-European extraction, but with a significant Asian minority.

Having established the broad characteristics of our audience we can now examine in detail the impact a selection of stories might have. Take the following list of items which typifies the sort of material that crops up in the in-tray of any small rural newsroom:

Council moves offices
Cholera epidemic in India
Police call to be armed
Local cholera outbreak
Dog rescues drowning boy
Average fish harvest in Iceland
New treatment for baldness
Local factory creates hundred jobs

In assessing the newsworthiness of each of these stories, it should be remembered that, given the same degree of change, stories with negative implications for people's security will have more impact than those with positive implications. These items in turn are more likely to attract the attention of the audience than those which contain only a degree of change.

Council moves offices

- It's not often that councils move offices. On the other hand, the impact of that change on the audience is likely to be minimal, other than causing minor confusion among the minority of the population who find cause to regularly call on council officers. We can therefore say that the change element in the story is Medium, but its impact on the audience, the amount of Security Concern it creates, will be Low.

Cholera epidemic in India

- Epidemics of disease are, sadly, not unusual in India, so the element of change is Low. If sufficient people are affected, the sheer scale of the problem may be sufficiently unusual to upgrade the status of the story to Medium. In terms of impact on the audience, that section of the audience which has few connections with Asia will find the news of passing interest only; if they have no links with India, and therefore little knowledge of the area or its people, the story will fall outside their boundary of relevance. On the other hand, listeners, viewers or readers with close ties with the sub-continent, and more specifically the exact area, will be extremely concerned - friends and even relations may be affected. The story will fall within their boundary of relevance and the degree of security concern will accordingly be High (-).

Police call to be armed

- In Britain the police are not armed, and continually resist suggestions that they should carry guns. Any such call by a senior police officer not only carries a High degree of change, it also carries considerable implications for the security of the audience. Not only is an icon of constancy (the Police as guarantor of law and order) apparently weakening, there is a direct perceived threat to the security of all individual members of the audience. The only caveat which might persuade us to reduce the degree of security concern from High to Medium/ High (-) is the absence of current and active threat. The break down of law and order remains potential at this stage.

Local cholera outbreak

- Not only is cholera rare in Britain, it is highly contagious and doesn't distinguish between victims. Thus there is a High level of change from the status quo, and a considerable and immediate threat to individual members of the audience, their families and the community as a whole. The degree of security concern is unequivocally High (-).

Dog rescues drowning boy

- This is the sort of 'ah' story which interests audiences, often as an 'and finally' item'. There is a High degree of change as we don't expect animals to show such intelligence or devotion. There is also a certain amount of social interest: dogs have an unusually close symbiotic relationship with man and are therefore included within many people's family group. We can therefore grant a small element of positive security concern in that the audience will feel the dog's action confirms and reinforces the validity of this special relationship.

Average fish harvest in Iceland

- The status of its fish harvest is unlikely to have an impact on an audience which has few connections with Iceland, especially as there is no change in the status quo.

New treatment for baldness

- Like many medical breakthroughs, a treatment for a previously untreatable condition carries a High element of change. However, as baldness doesn't affect everyone, and is ego- rather than life- threatening, the story carries only a Low to Medium(+) implication for the security of the audience.

Local factory creates hundred jobs

- The creation of a hundred jobs is obviously a change from the status quo. The degree of change will depend on whether the area is economically depressed, and whether the economy itself is in boom or recession. Let us say for the purposes of the exercise the degree of change in this case is High. The implications for the audience will depend on the broader significance of the story as well as its specific impact. Members of the audience actively seeking work in that area will obviously be considerably interested in the story, so the impact will be Medium (+). But even people with no intention of working for the company may still find the story interesting because the positive implications of the story for an economy in recession will have a wider relevance.

We can now list the elements of Change and Security Concern contained in each story:

	Security	
Item	Change	Concern
Council moves offices	Medium	Low
Cholera epidemic-India	Low/Medium	Low/High (-)*
Police call to be armed	High	Med/High (-)*
Cholera outbreak-local	High	High (-)*
Dog rescues boy	High	Low (+)*
Icelandic fish harvest	None	None
Treatment for baldness	High	Low/Med (+)*
Factory creates jobs	High	Medium (+)*

Stories marked with an asterisk (*) will have the highest impact on our target audience and should therefore be selected for inclusion in the news.

Selecting specialist stories

The selection of specialist stories, especially those with a scientific, technical or economic content, can cause problems for journalists. This is because the audience, and quite possibly the reporter, has no familiarity with the issues or concepts involved, so cannot immediately judge the story's significance.

Scientific stories, discoveries and developments are bound to be news: by definition they involve something new, a change from the status quo. The more difficult question is whether that change will be perceived as relevant by the audience.

The discovery of a technically significant but otherwise complex and obscure chemical process may excite scientists, but it is unlikely to provoke reaction from a general audience. Quite simply, a general audience wants to know only what, if any, impact the development will have on their daily lives. That perceived relevance varies according to subject. To take an extreme example, a new cure for cancer will carry more radical implications for the audience than the development of a new mathematical theorem. Using perceived relevance as a guide we can draw up a 'league table' of the sciences and their intrinsic interest for the audience:

57

Subject	Perceived Relevance
Medicine	High
Life sciences (e.g. Psychology)	High
Nuclear energy	Med/high
Engineering	Medium
Physics	Med/low
Chemistry	Med/low
Astronomy	Low
Mathematics	Low

Note that the important consideration here is the relevance the audience attaches to the subject, not its intrinsic significance.

For instance, the person in the street is unlikely to be familiar with nuclear physics, and won't therefore be interested in technical developments *per se*. But developments in the nuclear power industry will be of greater general interest, simply because of the continuing debate over safety: there is a profound level of fundamental security concern.

In the same way, the products of both physics and chemistry are important in our daily lives, but the public is technophobic about the sciences themselves.

Pure mathematics is not only an arcane subject which few people understand, it is also perceived as having no intrinsic relevance to the public. To a certain extent that is also true of astronomy, although in this case the audience can at least grasp the broad principles of developments without getting bogged down in theory. For example, the element of change in the discovery of a new planet would be of general interest, even though the details of its discovery might be highly technical and beyond the understanding of the layperson.

There are ways in which the audience can be encouraged to change its perception of a subject's relevance and these will be explained in the next section.

Content Selection

Even though a story may have been selected as potentially newsworthy, the way in which it is written can make all the difference to whether or not it catches the attention of the audience. One of the secrets of good news writing is to make the most of the material available, and that includes presenting the various elements of the story in such a way that they grip the audience.

It is generally accepted that every story has six elements which, if they are all included, illuminate every facet of the event or issue. These elements are:

Who
What
Why
Where
When
How

In every story, one of these elements will be more important than the others. For example, if a man bites a dog it's the nature of the event, 'What', which is most striking and unusual. If an acrobat cooks a meal on a high wire stretched across a ravine, it's the location, the 'Where' (or one might argue the 'Why'!), of the event which is important. Other details are secondary to the most significant aspect of the event.

The traditional 'story teller', or *Chronological Narrative*, format recounts the various aspects of an event in the order in which they happened. (See Figure 4, below.)

Figure 4

Beginning -- > End

The disadvantage of this style is that the point of the story may become buried, or be so long in coming that the audience loses interest.

The *Inverted Pyramid* format (Figure 5, below) used in most British and American newsrooms gets round this problem by giving precedence to the most significant factor. This is called the *Lead*, or 'news angle'. Supporting facts and details are then added in declining order of importance. For example:

Figure 5

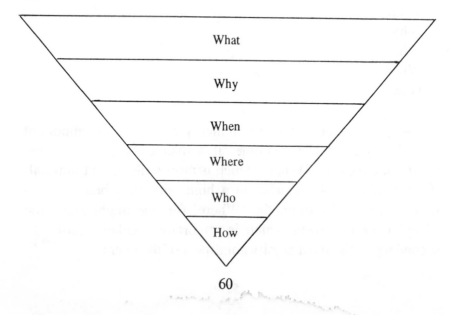

The Lead forms a lens through which the audience views the rest of the story, it:

"... focuses the story in a particular direction...until a journalist finds out what to lead the story with, the story remains unfocused."[51]

The importance of the lead in broadcast news cannot be over-stated. The top line of each story has to serve the same function as the newspaper headline, grabbing the attention of the audience. But, unlike the headline, the lead has to flow seamlessly into the rest of the story.

Selecting the right lead is therefore crucial, but journalists may not be sure which point of the story is the most significant.

The simple answer is to highlight that element of change in the story which will generate most security concern, or, if there is no security concern, the element of greatest novelty or social interest.

To illustrate this point with an example, let's look at the following notes of a local authority meeting, which have been written in chronological order:

Chief Constable Derek Hedges arrived late for the Police Authority meeting, explaining that his car appeared to have been stolen. Presenting his report, he told members of the Committee that there had been 30,000 crimes in the county last year. The largest number of offences involved car theft, closely followed by burglary and drugs. The number of incidents involving fire-arms had increased to

500 this year as against 100 in the previous year. Mr Hedges said in answer to a question that he was urging the Home Office to allow police to carry guns to protect themselves and the public, as without them the police were fighting a losing battle against organised crime. He paid tribute to his officers and pressed the committee for a twenty five percent increase in manpower to cope with the rise in the number of offences.

The surprising and disturbing facet of the report is the threat that police will lose their battle against crime unless officers are allowed to carry guns. This is the most significant angle of the story, judged in terms of both change and security concern. But, in its present form, the report doesn't make this clear. The story has to be rewritten in 'inverted pyramid' form, giving due emphasis to the most important point:

A senior policeman has told the government that his officers will have to be armed [change] if they're to win the fight against organised crime [security concern]. Chief Constable Derek Hedges today reported to the county council's Police Committee that there had been a five fold increase in the number of incidents involving firearms over the last year. He said that he had warned the Home Office that unless officers are allowed to carry guns, the police would not be able to protect the public.

Written in this way the crux of the story is immediately obvious to the audience.

The supporting details of the story should also be ordered in terms of their change and security concern. In the example above, the second and third sentences push home and flesh out the relevance of the security threat to the audience. If we wished to extend the report, the reporter could include additional information about the incidence of crime, the level of car-theft and drugs offences, and the need for more officers.

Had the content of the Chief Constable's report been more mundane and carried less threat to the security of the audience, the fact that his own car had been stolen would have qualified as the lead. There is a strong element of change, in that we don't expect senior police officers to have their cars stolen, and an element of social interest: the humbling of a member of the power élite allows us to re-assess positively our own social position.

Writing specialist stories

Sorting out the priorities of a story's constituent elements is relatively straightforward when the issues and events involved are familiar to both audience and journalist. The difficulty once again comes when handling a complex story which involves science, technology, economics or indeed any field in which a general audience (and reporter) cannot be expected to understand the details or their context.

The first and very important point to grasp is that, unless the audience has specialised knowledge, it must be assumed that technical details will not capture attention. A general audience simply won't have the bench-marks it needs to assess the impact of the story. The significance of the story, both in terms of change and security concern, therefore need to be expressed in terms the audience can understand:

63

Use everyday analogies

- Specialist details should be explained using familiar analogies.(e.g. "a Black Hole behaves something like the plug-hole in your bath.")

Spell out the everyday implications of the story

- Highlight the benefits or drawbacks of the story for a general audience. For example, the development of a new chemical will be of no interest to a general audience, but the potential benefits will: e.g., "This new chemical means longer engine life for your car". Few people understand the chemistry of the upper atmosphere. But the practical implications of the interaction between CFCs and the ozone layer can be readily understood: "If the hole in the ozone layer continues to get bigger, one in every five sun-bathers on the beach at Brighton could have skin cancer by the end of the century".

Avoid (or explain) jargon

- There are three types of jargon: *word, concept* and *procedural*. All three should be avoided if the journalist wants to keep the attention of the audience, but it is easier in some cases than others.

WORD JARGON

- In many fields specific words have developed into a language that suits the specialist demands of that discipline, but will mean little to anyone else. If a general audience is to understand the story, specialist terms need to be translated into everyday words with the same meaning.

CONCEPT JARGON

- In some cases the concepts involved in a technical story are so obtuse or complex that they will mean little to a general audience, even if couched in everyday terms. This particularly applies to some scientific subjects like cosmology and quantum mechanics, where the context of the story can be as difficult to understand as the details of the story itself. In some cases it is possible to get round this problem by spending a short time explaining the background before launching into the details. More usually, it will be easier to abandon the story: if nobody is going to understand it, why do it!

PROCEDURAL JARGON

- This is often used by bureaucrats or workers in large organisations, who seem to find the procedural path a policy or decision follows more interesting than the decision itself. The audience isn't interested in such internal details, so these should be avoided unless they are a fundamental aspect of the story.

Use 'picture' words

- Where possible use words which evoke an everyday image. For instance, 'Black Hole' is more evocative than 'singularity'; it's easier to visualise a 'Test Tube Baby' than 'in-vitro fertilisation'. As audience researcher Barrie Gunter points out in his study of audience receptiveness:

" Words that readily evoke images are better remembered than more abstract ones, because they provide better conceptual pegs on which information can be hung and more readily retrieved." [52]

Using these techniques, even the most technical story can be re-told in a form which the public can understand. Consider the following extract from a paper which appeared in a specialist medical research journal:

"Alzheimer's disease, which is characterised by amyloid plaques and neurofibrillary tangles, may be attributed to the abnormal expression of genes located on human chromosome 21. Genetic linkage studies have narrowed the region of candidate genes to 21q11.2-21q22 of the long arm of the chromosome. Several single copy sequences within this region, including the amyloid precursor protein, have been mapped to mouse chromosome 16. However, the consequences of developmental overexpression of genes on chromosome 16 have not been previously investigated because of the lethal effects of this aneuploidy during gestation. In the present report, we employ neural transplantation to study long term survival and pathogenesis in Trisomy 16 central nervous system tissues..."[53]

This turned out to be a very interesting story with real implications for the audience, but the original research paper, while decipherable by a scientist, would mean absolutely nothing to a layperson. Translated into 'everyday speak', and with a little extra questioning of the author, the implications of the passage to the general public become clear:

Genetically engineered mice are helping scientists crack the secrets of Alzheimer's disease, a distressing condition which causes irreversible brain damage in some older people. The disease is triggered by the build up of protein in brain cells, but scientists haven't been able to find out why this happens because they can't take brain samples from living patients. Now, by altering its genetic 'blueprint' they've been able to breed a special mouse which develops Alzheimer's disease in the same way as humans. Studies of the animals' brain tissue will allow researchers to track the early development of the illness, and could eventually lead to new and improved methods of treatment.

Simple everyday words replace the jargon, concepts are rendered clearly in a way that people will understand, and the relevance of the story to the security of the audience is spelled out.

The preceding two sections are equally relevant to both print and broadcast journalists, but there is another field which can cause particular headaches for radio journalists: the ordering of stories in a news bulletin.

Compiling a news bulletin

Ranking stories in order of priority can be a problem. The solution once again is to evaluate the relative strengths of change and security concern embodied in each.

It should be remembered that, given the same degree of

change, stories with negative implications for people's security are going to have more impact than those with positive implications. These items, in turn, are more likely to attract the attention of the audience than those which contain only a degree of change.

With these provisos in mind, it is a simple matter to establish the relative news values of the stories in the earlier example by re-ordering them:

Item	Security	
	Change	Concern
Cholera outbreak- local	High	High (-)*
Cholera epidemic- India	Low/Med	Low/High (-)*
Police call to be armed	High	Med/High(-) *
Factory creates jobs	High	Medium(+) *
Treatment for baldness	High	Low/Med(+) *
Dog rescues boy	High	Low(+) *
Council moves offices	Medium	Low
Icelandic fish harvest	None	None

The final running order for a six-item bulletin would therefore look like this:

Bulletin Item   **Story**

1   Cholera outbreak- local
2   Cholera epidemic- India
3   Police call to be armed
4   Factory creates jobs
5   Treatment for baldness
6   Dog rescues boy

The inclusion of the Indian cholera story at second position may seem anomalous in view of the low degree of change. It can, however, be justified on three counts. Firstly, the story will carry a considerable security concern for a Asian minority audience, and this interest should be catered for. Secondly, there may be direct links between the two outbreaks, and even though the journalist may not be able to say as much, it would be wise to 'signpost' the possibility by physically placing the two stories together in the bulletin. The third reason is technical: a bulletin's flow can be improved by the use of themes, grouping similar stories if their newsworthiness is not too different.

CHAPTER 7

SUMMARY

Someone once cynically defined journalism as the art of extracting information from people who don't want to talk and giving it to people who don't want to listen.

The reporter's job is not only to dig up the facts, but also to present them in such a way that the public *does* want to listen, or watch, or read. To do that effectively requires an understanding of the factors which determine the impact of news on the audience, and, just as importantly, it requires a knowledge of the influences which will at some stage shape the reporter's news judgement.

Firstly, there are the operational constraints of the news process. Availability of resources, pressures on time and the logistics of coverage are just a few of the practical factors which decide whether a story is covered.

Secondly, the way journalists interpret news depends heavily on the collective norms of their professional environment and the society in which they live and work.

Thirdly, news judgements can be affected by outside pressures. The power and influence of the media make journalists an attractive target for establishment and non-established groups seeking to encourage news consumers to interpret the world in a particular way.

Fourthly, the way we use language can dictate the way both journalists and audience interpret stories.

Models of news evaluation based on these factors alone are incomplete: they explain how the news process works, they don't explain why it works. Nor do they enable journalists to predict the impact of a story on the audience as a whole. Journalists and analysts alike have failed to take into account the interests and needs of the public, simply because of the apparent impossibility of assessing the requirements of a mass listener- or reader- ship.

This problem can be overcome by establishing basic factors which motivate attention in all individual members of the audience.

Recent anthropological research suggests that humans are preconditioned to be aware of uncertainty in the environment. This is a survival mechanism which gives the individual a chance to pre-empt change which threatens to adversely affect its physical or social security. We are programmed with a deep seated instinct to monitor for change in our environment and to evaluate that change for its possible impact on our lives. If an event contains change which is relevant to the security of the audience, it will attract attention.

It can be argued that change and security concern are primary conditions for newsworthiness. Other factors such as operational, structural and socio-political influences are of secondary importance. They may well affect the selection and presentation of news, but they will not generate audience attention unless the primary conditions are met.

Using such a model the journalist can predict precisely the impact of a story on a given audience. That means stories can be chosen, written and ordered so they have relevance to the audience. This not only gives meaning to the function of the news process (no small matter), it also gives journalists a way of ensuring their work has the 'bite' which can mean the difference between 'lead story' or front page prominence, and down-page or down-bulletin oblivion.

GLOSSARY

Affiliated community   An external group which is 'adopted' by a community and brought within its boundary of relevance (qv).

Air time   The time available for a radio or TV broadcast.

Boundary of relevance   Point beyond which an audience will not regard a story as relevant.

Breaking story   A story which is beginning to unfold; an event which is starting to happen.

Bulletin   Selection of stories which make up a news broadcast.

Causality   The operation of cause and effect.

Change   A primary condition for newsworthiness (qv).

Chronological Narrative   A news writing format (qv) which sets out the elements of a story in the order that they happened.

Codes   Conventions of language which determine how signs (qv) are interpreted.

73

Collective norms	Behaviour, views and ideas which are common to a social or professional group.
Comparative news evaluation	The assessment of the news value (qv) of one news story relative to a another.
Competition	Media compete to get to a new story first.
Composition	Some stories may be selected purely to balance a page or bulletin.
Connotative curtain	Use of myths (qv) to hide the reality of a situation.
Consonance	Tendency to select and process news in accordance with the journalists' pre-conceptions and expectations.
Continuity	Once a story is in the news, coverage is likely to continue.
Co-optation	The adoption of one story to complement another.
Copy taster	A journalist whose job is to assess the potential newsworthiness of material coming into a newsroom.
Élite nations	Nations with political or economic power in the international community.
Élite people	People with social standing and power in a community.

Establishment	Influential groups and individuals who determine the collective norms (qv) and policy of a state.
Format	The way in which a story is written.
Frequency	The speed with which the news process recycles. Radio news happens every hour, a monthly magazine comes out every four weeks.
Icon of constancy	Symbol of stability which reassures people. An icon may be physical, like a familiar landmark; social, like the Royal Family; or psychological, like religious belief.
Inverted Pyramid	A news writing format which orders the elements of a story in their order of importance, the most significant first.
Jargon	*Word*: specialist words used as a form of communication within specific fields. *Concept*: specialist concepts encountered in highly complex fields, especially science. *Procedural*: technical terms which relate to bureaucratic procedures or decision-making processes.

Lead	The most significant element in a story (also called the 'news angle').
Lead story	The first story in a radio or TV bulletin, or the main story on a newspaper page.
Lead time	The time it takes to prepare a magazine or other literature for publication.
Logistics	Organisation of technical resources and transport.
Machiavelli, Nicolo	16th century political observer whose writings laid bare the devious and manipulative reality of power politics.
Machiavellian hypothesis	Theory that human intelligence developed to cope with the complexities of social interaction within groups.
Meaningfulness	An event is more likely to be covered if it has relevance to the journalist.
Media analysis	Study of the way the way the media works.
Myth	Collection of signs (qv) which acquire conceptual values not actually related to their conventional root meaning.

Negativity	Negative news is more frequently covered than good news.
Neoteny	The process by which some animals retain aspects of infantile development into adulthood.
News evaluation	The process of assessing the importance, or significance, of a news story, see news value (qv).
News value	The importance, or significance, of a news story, assessed either in terms of its potential impact on the audience, or its attraction for the journalist.
Newsworthiness	Alternative word for news value (qv).
Nose for news	The art of making news judgements by instinct rather than rational analysis.
Operational factors	Aspects of the news operation which affect journalists' judgements.
Pædomorphism	Treating something else, for instance an animal, as if it were a human child.
Perceived relevance	What people see as relevant. This may or may not equate with true relevance.

Personalisation	Events are represented in terms of the people involved.
Picture word	Literally, a word or words which can be drawn as a picture. For instance, Test Tube baby.
Pluralistic society	Society in which various groups influence and affect the governing process.
Predictability	An event is more likely to be covered if it is prescheduled.
Prefabrication	Stories which are already half written will receive preference.
Referent	Something against which other things are judged.
Rolling story	A story which has broken (qv) and is still on-going.
Scale	The size of an event. The bigger the story the more likely it is to be covered.
Security concern	The concern an individual or group has for its physical, social or psychological security. A primary condition for newsworthiness (qv).
Semiotics	The study of the social production and communication of meaning.
Significance	Relevance of a story to the security concerns (qv) of the audience.

Signifier	Part of a sign (qv); an arbitrary symbol used to denote a concept.
Signified	Part of a sign (qv); the concept denoted by a signifier (qv).
Signs	A symbol used to communicate concepts. *See* signifier and signified (qv).
Status quo	The way things are before they change.
Structural factors	Aspects of the way a news organisation is run which affect the judgements made by staff.
Symbiosis	A relationship, often between two different animal species, which is based on mutual benefit. For instance, dogs offer humans loyalty, affection and protection in exchange for shelter and food.
Technophobia	Aversion to technology and complicated machinery.
Temporal models	Means of calculating the future implications of past and present actions.
Unambiguity	Events which are straightforward and easy to understand will be chosen for coverage in preference to awkward or complex stories.

| **Unexpectedness** | The more unusual or unexpected the event the more likely it is to be covered. |
| **Xenophobia** | Dislike of strangers. |

FURTHER READING
and BIBLIOGRAPHY

Bell, A. (1991) *The Language of News Media* Blackwell
Written by a journalist who is also a linguist, this book offers a comprehensive study of the influence of language on decision-making in the news process.

Billig, M. (1992) *Talking of the Royal Family* Routledge
Rather than sit in his study Billig went out to find out what real people think of the Royals. Interesting reading on a public obsession often referred to but rarely analysed.

Boyd, A. (1993) *Broadcast Journalism* Focal Press
This is regarded by many as the standard broadcast journalism textbook. A comprehensive and well written practical guide to the techniques of radio and television news, though it contains little on the analysis of news.

Byrne, R./Whiten, A. (1988) *Machiavellian Intelligence* Clarendon Press
A collection of essays by experts who support the Machiavellian intelligence hypothesis. A bit specialist for the non-scientist, but offers a fascinating insight into ape (and human) behaviour for those willing to make the effort. Essential reading for those who wish to delve deeper into the anthropological model put forward in this book.

Cheney, D./Seyfarth, R. (1990) *How Monkeys See the World* Chicago University Press
Specialist work on the behaviour of ververt monkeys. Intended for primatologists, this work extends and expands the authors' contribution to Machiavellian Intelligence (above). Interesting, but heavy going for the general reader.

Cohen, S./Young, J. (1973) (eds) *The Manufacture of News: Deviance, Social Problems and the Mass Media* Constable
A collection of essays notable mainly for Galtung and Ruge's classic study of comparative news evaluation.

Franken, R. (1988) *Human Motivation* Brooks/Cole
There are many books on motivation, and this is perhaps not the easiest (or cheapest) introduction to the field, as it's aimed at psychologists with prior knowledge.

Gans, H. (1980) *Deciding What's News* Constable
Regarded as a standard textbook, especially in the United States. Worth reading if you can get hold of a copy.

Gunter, B. (1987) *Poor Reception* Lawrence Erlbaum
An exhaustive study of audience response to news, written by an expert. Worth dipping into, but too specialist for the general reader.

Hartley, J. (1982) *Understanding News* Routledge
Excellent and comprehensive introduction to semiotics and analysis of the content of news, although jargon and a very 'sociological' style make this book a little heavy going at times. An essential read.

Hetherington, A. (1985) *News, Newspapers & Television* Macmillan
Focuses on the decision makers in the news process, and the factors which influence their judgements. The author was a senior journalist and editor for many years, experience which is reflected in his common-sense approach to analysing the news process.

Morris, D. (1977) *The Naked Ape* Triad Grafton
The original best-seller. Morris puts man under the zoologist's microscope to find out how human behaviour can be explained by our animal past. A bit dated in style, and theory has moved on since the sixties when it was first published, but still fascinating.

Pilger, J. (1992) *Distant Voices* Vintage
Depending on your viewpoint, a masterful and courageous exposé of the influence of power politics on journalism, or the paranoid outpourings of a militant liberal. This book should be read by every aspiring, and working, journalist.

Schlesinger, P. (1987) *Putting 'Reality' Together* Methuen
Schlesinger spent seven years observing what goes on in BBC newsrooms. There's therefore not a lot left unsaid about the operational and structural factors which affect journalists' news judgement. This book is essential reading for anyone about to start work in a BBC newsroom.

Serpell, J. (1986) *In the Company of Animals* Blackwell
Serpell specialises in researching just why people, and the English in particular, are potty about animals. Easy and interesting to read.

Skinner, Q. (1981) *Machiavelli* Oxford University Press
Nicolo Machiavelli was a 16th century political observer who has been 'black-balled' by history for spelling out how it helps to be nasty and devious if you want to get on in politics. There are many works on Machiavelli. This one has the virtue of being short and fairly easy to read.

Wallis, R./Baran, S. (1990) *The Known World of Broadcast News* Routledge
The authors, an academic and a journalist, examine how changes in the world of broadcasting are affecting the news process and the world view presented by journalists.

REFERENCES

1   Familiar Quotations Bartlett 14th ed. 1968 p.808b
2   Alastair Hetherington (Macmillan 1985) *News,
    Newspapers and Television* p.4
3   Hetherington p.2
4   Hetherington p.8
5   Hetherington p.10
6   Johan Galtung and Mari Ruge "Structuring and Selecting
    News", in Cohen and Young (Constable 1973) *The
    Manufacture of News: Deviance, Social Problems and
    the Mass Media* pp.62-71
7   Allan Bell (Blackwell 1991) *The Language of News
    Media* p.159
8   Philip Schlesinger (Methuen 1987) *Putting 'Reality'
    Together* pp.83-105
9   Schlesinger p.60
10 Schlesinger p.60
11 Schlesinger p.51
12 Bell p.159
13 Bell p.59
14 Schlesinger p.135
15 Schlesinger pp.106-134, and Hetherington p.38
16 Roger Wallis and Stanley Baran (Routledge 1990) *The
    Known World of Broadcast News* p.7
17 Wallis and Baran p.217
18 John Pilger (Vintage 1992) *Distant Voices* p.85
19 Wallis and Baran p.209
20 John Hartley (Routledge 1982) *Understanding News* p.9

21   Hartley p.9
22   Hartley p.80
23   Hartley p.26
24   Hartley p.28
25   Bell pp.157-8
26   Bell p.156
27   Schlesinger p.107
28   Bell p.89
29   Hartley p.148
30   Herbert Gans (Constable 1980) *Deciding What's News* p.234
31   Hetherington p.38
32   Schlesinger p.119
33   Schlesinger p.106
34   Bell p.232
35   Robert Franken (Brooks/Cole) *Human Motivation* p.55
36   Hetherington p.10
37   Desmond Morris (Triad 1977) *The Naked Ape* p.20; *see* also Thomas Wynn "Tools and the evolution of human intelligence", in Richard Byrne and Andrew Whiten (Clarendon 1988) *Machiavellian Intelligence* p.272.
38   Nicholas Humphrey, "The social function of intellect", in Byrne and Whiten p.17-18
39   Byrne and Whiten p.4
40   Dorothy Cheney and Robert Seyfarth, "Social and non-social knowledge in ververt monkeys", in Byrne and Whiten p.268
41   Frans de Waal, "Chimpanzee politics", in Byrne and Whiten pp.122-131; *see* also Sue Savage-Rumbaugh and Kelly McDonald, "Deception and social manipulation in symbol-using apes", in Byrne and Whiten pp.224-237

42 James Serpell (Blackwell 1986) *In the Company of Animals* p.64
43 Bell p.233
44 Hetherington p.40
45 Bell p.156
46 Hartley p.83
47 Peter Berger and Thomas Luckmann "The Social Construction of Reality" (Penguin 1966), cited in Hartley p.139
48 Bell p.204
49 Pilger p.4
50 Michael Billig (Routledge 1992) *Talking of the Royal Family* p.222
51 Bell p.152
52 Barrie Gunter (Lawrence Erlbaum 1987) *Poor Reception* p.71
53 Sarah-Jane Richards *et al*, "Transplants of mouse trisomy 16 hippocampus provide a model of Alzheimer's disease neuropathology" The EMBO Journal (1991) vol.10 No.2 pp.297-303

INDEX

G = Glossary entry

People in Organisations - 4th edition

Pat Armstrong & Chris Dawson

A well-written introduction to the management of people at work, used by many colleges on BTEC HNC/D Business Studies, Stage 1 DMS, IPM, IWM, and the new certificates and diplomas in management.
Contents include:
Organisational goals/structure/systems/change
Human resource planning
Personality/attitude formation & change
Motivation & rewards/communication & perception
Groups & leadership
Recruitment, selection, testing, learning & training
Industrial relations & legislation
Book - ISBN 0 946139 55 5   320 pages   paperback
Tutor's Manual - simulated company + 10 exercises, OHPs, notes & materials for class use to support/extend the book.   Copying rights.
ISBN 0 946139 60 1   A4 looseleaf binder

Human Resources Management

Terry McIlwee & Ivor Roberts

Human Resources Management is both a new text in its own right and the third edition of **Personnel Management in Context** - the popular introduction to personnel management set in its organisational and national context
Contents include: -
The business environment; structure of corporate objectives; major functions of enterprise - marketing, production, the function of management; total quality management; the UK political system; the labour market in the UK; the Government and the labour market; unemployment; the British system of industrial relations.
ISBN 1 85450 022 8 - 454pp.

Accounting & Finance

Humphrey Shaw

Strategic Financial Management

In an increasingly hostile global marketplace, a firm's ability to manage finances well is crucial. This book takes a highly innovative approach to the full range of strategic issues. Using U.S. & U.K. examples, it has a critical review of accepted financial management theories & evaluation techniques, showing how they fit into a total strategic management framework.
Book (pbk) 300pp. ISBN 1 85450 042 2

Finance in Organisations

An introduction, for the not-so-numerate, to the financial aspects of management in organisations. Diagrams, charts, company accounts & clear explanations of the main methods of understanding & controlling the finances of a business.
Book - pbk, ISBN 1 85450 019 8 **Tutor's Manual** - worked/tested exercises (class use or free-standing 2-day course for managers new to the subject) ISBN 1 85450 031 7 **Projection Pack** of 44 OHPs to support book/tutor's manual ISBN 1 85450 037 6

Finance & Accounting: cases & problems

150 problems and cases on financial accounting & control from first steps to medium difficulty. 150 cases and problems in financial management specially written for the person studying the subject from first steps to medium difficulty. Examples span a range of industries, including hotel & catering & leisure. With answers. ISBN 1 85450 087 2

Decision Making

40 case studies in financial & quantitative management. With common accounting ratios, prescribed formats for company accounts, glossary & DCF/NPV tables. **Book** ISBN 0 946139 42 3
Tutor's Manual (worked answers, notes, OHPs) ISBN 0 946139 47 4

Entrepreneurial Decision Making

50 case studies on small & medium-sized businesses, with crucial decisions to make. Glossary; DCF tables; cases on Individual, Business Environment & Enterprise, Organisational, Marketing & Financial decisions.
Book ISBN 0 946139 69 5
Tutor's Manual - answers, notes, OHPs ISBN 0 946139 74 1